Understanding

PRESIDENTIAL APPOINTMENTS

Amanda Peterson

PowerKiDS press.

New York

Published in 2018 by **The Rosen Publishing Group, Inc.**
29 East 21st Street, New York, NY 10010

Cataloging-in-Publication Data

Names: Peterson, Amanda.
Title: Understanding presidential appointments / Amanda Peterson.
Description: New York : PowerKids Press, 2018. | Series: What's up with your government? |
    Includes index.
Identifiers: LCCN ISBN 9781538323304 (pbk.) | ISBN 9781538322345 (library bound) |
    ISBN 9781538323311 (6 pack)
Subjects: LCSH: United States--Officials and employees--Selection and appointment. |
    Government executives--Selection and appointment--United States.
Classification: LCC JK421.P49 2018 | DDC 352.30973--dc23

First Edition

Developed and Produced by Focus Strategic Communications, Inc.
    Project Manager: Adrianna Edwards
    Editor: Ron Edwards
    Design and Composition: Ruth Dwight
    Copy editors: Adrianna Edwards, Francine Geraci
    Media Researchers: Adrianna Edwards, Paula Joiner
    Proofreader: Francine Geraci
    Index: Ron Edwards, Maddi Nixon

Photo Credits: Credit Abbreviations: LOC Library of Congress; S Shutterstock, Position on
the page: T: top, B: Bottom, C: Center, L: left, R: right. Cover TL: Abbie Rowe. White House
Photographs. John F. Kennedy Presidential Library and Museum, Boston, TR: Lima Junior/S,
CL: Carsten Reisinger/S, B: amadeustx/S; 1 TL: Abbie Rowe. White House Photographs.
John F. Kennedy Presidential Library and Museum, Boston, TR: Lima Junior/S, CL: Carsten
Reisinger/S; 4: Hasan Shaheed/S; 5: photo_master2000/S; 6: 360b/S 7: Drop of Light/S; 8:
Everett - Art/S; 9 TL: LOC/LC-DIG-ppmsca-31804, TR, C, BR: Everett Historical/S, BL:
LOC/LC-D43-T01-9885; 10: LOC/LC-H22-D- 4579; 11: stock_photo_world/S; 12: everything
possible/S; 13: Rob Crandall/S; 14: andrey_l/S; 15: Mark Van Scyoc/S; 16: Official White House
Photo by Lawrence Jackson; 17: Christopher Halloran/S; 18: White House Official Photograph;
20, 21: a katz/S; 22 TL: Rawpixel.com/S, BL: Aleksandr Danilenko/S, R: Casper1774 Studio/S;
23: danielfela/S; 24: Andrey_Kuzmin/S; 25: Rob Crandall/S; 26: The Trump-Pence Transition
Team; 27: Rob Crandall/S; 28: a katz/S; 29: State Department photo by Michael Gross; Design
Elements: Nella/S, tassita numsri/S.

Manufactured in the United States of America

CPSIA Compliance Information: Batch BW18PK: For Further Information contact
Rosen Publishing, New York, New York at 1-800-237-9932.

CONTENTS

THE APPOINTMENT POWER

IMPORTANT ASSIGNMENTS

Has an adult ever trusted you with an important task? Maybe your teacher asked you to deliver a message to the school's office. Or perhaps your school's principal had you show a new student around your school. Students selected for special tasks are likely chosen because they demonstrate good leadership skills, are reliable, and work hard. When a person is assigned a job, it is sometimes called an **appointed** position.

Students who are reliable and hardworking are often selected by teachers to do special tasks.

FAST FACT

Sometimes students who demonstrate leadership qualities and responsibility are asked by teachers or principals to take on duties such as hall monitoring. Hall monitors keep order in school hallways and make sure that students show up to classes on time.

★ ★

PRESIDENTIAL APPOINTMENTS

There are many kinds of appointed positions. In the United States, the most important appointed positions are called presidential appointments. The people who work in appointed positions help the president do their job. They also make sure the president's ideas and opinions are spread throughout the government.

No Small Task

A new president must appoint people to over 4,000 positions! Filling the most important positions can take many months. Presidents-elect have staff to help them with the process. Former President Bill Clinton had almost 100 people helping with his appointments.

William Jefferson Clinton served as the 42nd president of the United States for two terms (1993–2001).

THE APPOINTMENT CLAUSE

The Founding Fathers gave the president many powers. They said the president could appoint people to some of the most important jobs in the **federal** government.

The part of the Constitution that covers presidential appointments is called the Appointment Clause (article 2, section 2, clause 2). It states that the president "shall nominate, and by and with the Advice and Consent of the Senate, shall appoint Ambassadors, other public Ministers and Consuls, Judges of the Supreme Court, and all other Officers of the United States."

President George W. Bush appointed Condoleezza Rice as secretary of state in 2005. She was the first African American woman to serve in that role. In 1933, Frances Perkins was the first woman to be appointed to the US cabinet, by President Franklin D Roosevelt.

ADVICE AND CONSENT

The Founding Fathers wanted the president to decide who helped run the government. But they also wanted to make sure the president made good choices. They said the Senate had to give advice and provide **consent**, or give approval, for these choices.

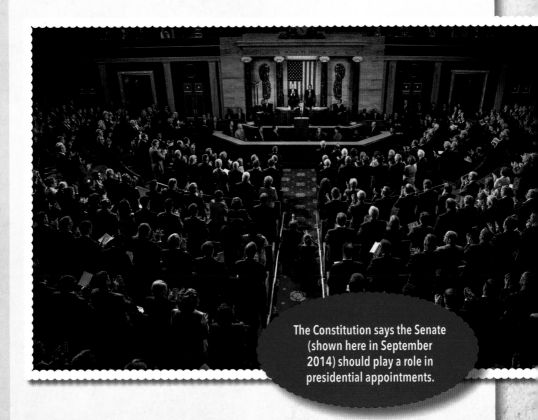

The Constitution says the Senate (shown here in September 2014) should play a role in presidential appointments.

FAST FACT

The Founding Fathers were part of the group that wrote the United States Constitution. The seven key figures were John Adams, Benjamin Franklin, Alexander Hamilton, John Jay, Thomas Jefferson, James Madison, and George Washington.

★ ★ ★ ★ ★ ★ ★ ★ ★ ★ ★ ★ ★ ★ ★ ★ ★ ★ ★

EARLY PRESIDENTIAL APPOINTMENTS

Under British rule, many government jobs were given to friends and family members. The Founding Fathers wanted presidential appointments to be fair. They believed a person's education and work experience should decide whether they worked in the government.

George Washington's own nephew, Bushrod Washington, asked to be appointed the US attorney for Virginia. Washington said no. He knew other lawyers were far more qualified to do the job.

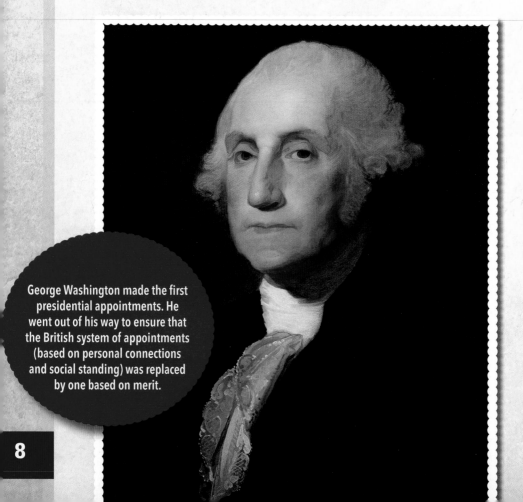

George Washington made the first presidential appointments. He went out of his way to ensure that the British system of appointments (based on personal connections and social standing) was replaced by one based on merit.

THE FIRST APPOINTMENTS

During the Revolutionary War, Washington met with
a group of **advisors**. He liked hearing their ideas
and opinions. They helped him make big decisions.
Washington appointed officers he knew could lead
their departments and make important decisions. As
president, Washington called his advisors his **cabinet**.
The first cabinet had only four **officers**.

EDMUND RANDOLPH
Attorney General

THOMAS JEFFERSON
Secretary of State

GEORGE
WASHINGTON

HENRY KNOX
Secretary of War

ALEXANDER HAMILTON
Secretary of the Treasury

"THE PRESIDENT NEEDS HELP"

ADDED APPOINTMENTS

Presidential appointments were once limited to judges, ambassadors, and department officers. But in 1937, the government said, "the president needs help." This resulted in the creation of many new appointed

positions. Louis Brownlow headed the committee that expanded the number of presidential appointments. Today, there are over 4,000 presidential appointees.

There are different types of presidential appointments. The highest positions require Senate approval. These appointments are called presidential appointments with Senate confirmation. Others do not need Senate approval.

Louis Brownlow (right), along with Charles E. Merriam, were two of the members of the President's Reorganization Committee. They are seen here on September 23, 1938, after meeting with President Franklin Roosevelt.

APPOINTMENTS WITHOUT SENATE APPROVAL

Many presidential appointments do not need Senate approval. These include senior executive service staff and Schedule C jobs.

SENIOR EXECUTIVE SERVICE

Senior executive service staff are often managers. These people report to appointees who do require Senate approval.

SCHEDULE C JOBS

Schedule C staff work in positions that handle confidential, or private, information. There are more than 1,400 Schedule C jobs, and they are considered the lowest level of political appointments. They are often used to reward volunteers who helped get the president elected.

Many of these positions that do not require Senate approval are in the White House, such as press secretaries, chiefs of staff, speech writers, and special advisors.

The press secretary is a presidential appointment that does not require approval from the Senate. Donald Trump appointed Sean Spicer as his press secretary in December 2016. Spicer resigned in July 2017.

APPOINTMENTS WITH SENATE APPROVAL

The most important presidential appointments require approval from the Senate. A study in 2012 found that there were as many as 1,400 positions appointed by the president that required Senate approval. Many of those jobs are in the Judicial Branch.

US ATTORNEYS

US attorneys represent the federal government in court. They help enforce federal laws throughout the country. There are 93 US attorneys appointed by the president.

US MARSHALS

US marshals help enforce federal laws. They make sure federal courtrooms are safe, arrest dangerous people, move prisoners, and protect witnesses. The 93 marshals are members of the United States Marshals Service (USMS).

FEDERAL JUDGES

Federal judges are appointed to federal courts of appeals or district courts. There are over 3,000 federal judges.

Judges and justices in the federal court system are presidential appointments that require Senate confirmation.

ATTORNEY GENERAL

The attorney general is the head of the Department of Justice. The person in this position is the highest-ranking lawyer in the federal government. The attorney general gives advice to the president and represents the US government in legal matters.

On February 9, 2017, Jeff Sessions, pictured here in 2005, became the 84th attorney general of the United States.

SUPREME COURT JUSTICES

Justices appointed to the US Supreme Court decide the most important court cases in the United States. There are nine judges known as justices—a chief justice and eight associate justices. They are nominated by the president and confirmed by Senate approval.

FAST FACT

The judicial branch makes sure that laws are followed. It is made up of a system of courts. The highest court is the Supreme Court.

★ ★ ★ ★ ★ ★ ★ ★ ★ ★ ★ ★ ★ ★ ★ ★ ★ ★ ★

AMBASSADORS

Ambassadors are the highest-ranking members of the US government who live and work in other countries. An ambassador helps US citizens living in that country, promotes the president's goals and policies, and attends important events on behalf of the US government. There are 265 representatives in 180 countries and other international agencies around the world.

Pictured here is the US embassy in Kiev, Ukraine, in 2015.

THE EMBASSY OF
THE UNITED STATES OF AMERICA
Посольство
Сполучених Штатів Америки

FAST FACT

The United States Foreign Service has about 300 embassies, consulates, and diplomatic missions around the world, employing nearly 50,000 individuals.

★ ★

HEADS OF INDEPENDENT AGENCIES

Hundreds of independent agencies and **commissions** carry out the work of the government. These agencies and commissions are, as their name implies, independent of presidential control. They are often led by a group instead of one person, and can serve for periods of time that may be longer than a president's term. Members of the group have different start and end dates. Presidents cannot remove agency heads from their positions.

Independent Agencies

Some of the independent agencies include the following. Do any of these names sound familiar?

- National Aeronautics and Space Administration (NASA)
- Central Intelligence Agency (CIA)
- United States Postal Service (USPS)
- Environmental Protection Agency (EPA)
- Federal Emergency Management Agency (FEMA)
- National Endowment for the Arts (NEA)
- Social Security Administration (SSA)
- Federal Trade Commission (FTC)

The Environmental Protection Agency (EPA) headquarters is located in this building in Washington, DC.

THE CABINET AND THE COURT

DEPARTMENT SECRETARIES

Fifteen departments report to the president, ranging from the State Department to the Department of Homeland Security. Fourteen of these are headed by secretaries, while the attorney general is in charge of the Department of Justice. These are some of the most important jobs in the federal government.

Members of Barack Obama's cabinet met with officials from Donald Trump's incoming administration on January 13, 2017.

FAST FACT

The 14 department secretaries and the attorney general are appointed by the president and become a central part of the federal cabinet.

★ ★

ADVISING THE PRESIDENT

The federal cabinet consists of the heads of the 15 federal departments as well as the vice president and other individuals the president wishes to include. The cabinet exists to advise and support the president, who relies on their knowledge and experience to make important decisions.

With the exception of the vice president, all cabinet members are appointed by the president. They hold their positions because the president trusts them to lead their departments and carry out the president's goals.

Trump's Cabinet

President Trump continued the tradition of predecessors to include individuals in his cabinet who worked in appointed positions that did not require Senate confirmation. The White House chief of staff and the heads of the Environmental Protection Agency and Small Business Administration are examples of such positions.

Reince Priebus was appointed the White House chief of staff in January 2017. He automatically became a member of President Trump's cabinet

SUPREME COURT

Many people consider Supreme Court appointments the most important decisions a president makes.

The US Supreme Court is the highest court in the land. Justices provide opinions on the most important court cases in the United States. Justices give the final word, and their decisions affect every citizen of the United States. They make sure the Constitution is upheld in the court system. The justices also make sure that no branch of the government abuses its power.

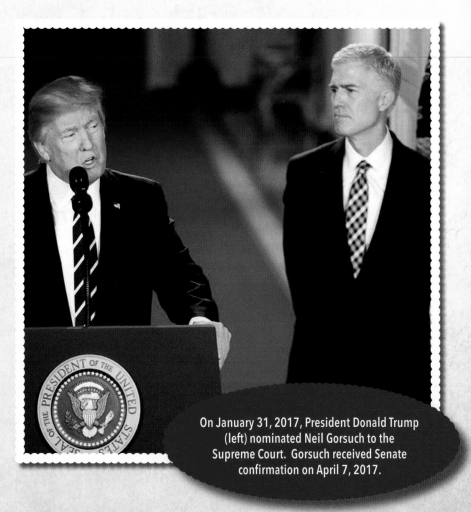

On January 31, 2017, President Donald Trump (left) nominated Neil Gorsuch to the Supreme Court. Gorsuch received Senate confirmation on April 7, 2017.

NAME	TITLE	YEAR APPOINTED	PRESIDENT WHO APPOINTED
John Roberts	Chief Justice	2005	George W. Bush
Anthony Kennedy	Associate Justice	1988	Ronald Reagan
Clarence Thomas	Associate Justice	1991	George H.W. Bush
Ruth Bader Ginsburg	Associate Justice	1993	Bill Clinton
Stephen Bryer	Associate Justice	1994	Bill Clinton
Samuel Alito	Associate Justice	2006	George W. Bush
Sonia Sotomayor	Associate Justice	2009	Barack Obama
Elena Kagan	Associate Justice	2010	Barack Obama
Neil Gorsuch	Associate Justice	2017	Donald Trump

FAST FACT

The Supreme Court Building is the headquarters of the court. The present building was completed in 1935 and is located in Washington, DC, across from the Capitol Building, home of the US Congress.

NOW HIRING

FILLING POSITIONS

Presidents make appointments throughout their terms. However, most are made right after they take office. New administrations must work quickly to fill positions. The president-elect needs a team that can to get to work immediately after they are **inaugurated**.

What do the president-elect and their advisors look for in candidates? They try to find people who are both qualified for the job and willing to push the president-elect's **agenda**.

President Donald Trump is shown here in November 2016 with Betsy DeVos, his nominee for secretary of education. She was confirmed in February 2017.

FAST FACT

The Senate vote on Betsy DeVos's cabinet nomination ended in a 50-50 split. It was the first time in history the vice president cast a tie-breaking vote on a cabinet nomination.

★ ★ ★ ★ ★ ★ ★ ★ ★ ★ ★ ★ ★ ★ ★ ★ ★ ★

SELECTING CANDIDATES

Sometimes the president-elect has someone in mind for a position. Other times, senators, members of Congress, Supreme Court justices, White House staff, interest groups, or lobbyists might make recommendations. The president-elect and their advisors determine the best candidates. They interview them and ask hard questions. When the president chooses a candidate for a position, the candidate's name is shared with the public.

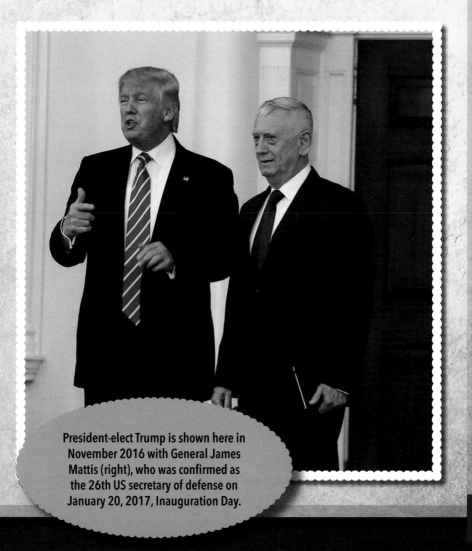

President-elect Trump is shown here in November 2016 with General James Mattis (right), who was confirmed as the 26th US secretary of defense on January 20, 2017, Inauguration Day.

THE NOMINATION PROCESS

The candidate for a presidential appointment must provide the government with many pieces of information. Fingerprints, tax records, medical records, several forms, and a document called the White House Personal Data Statement must be provided. The process is very demanding. Some of this information must be returned within 24 hours!

At the beginning of the appointment process, candidates must submit a staggering amount of information, including tax and medical records and fingerprints.

NO ROCK UNTURNED

The Federal Bureau of Investigation (FBI) uses the information to conduct a background check. This means that the FBI looks at every detail of a candidate's past. Agents even visit neighbors and ask questions. They leave no rock unturned! If the candidate passes the FBI's background check, they are given national security clearance.

The next step involves investigations from the Internal Revenue Service (IRS) and Office of Government Ethics (OGE). They review the candidate's background and consider conflicts of interest.

The FBI is an agency of the Department of Justice. It investigates past conduct of all nominees ranging from unpaid taxes to criminal offenses.

OFFICIAL NOMINATION

When candidates pass their background checks, they become nominees. Their names are written on a something called a "nomination parchment." This document includes the names of the candidates' home states, the positions they are nominated for, and the persons they will succeed.

The nomination parchment is put in an envelope, which is sealed with wax. The envelope is given to the Senate while it is in session. The candidate is now a nominee.

Wax Seals

People have been using wax to seal letters and documents since the time of the Romans. This was meant to keep these documents private and confidential. Wax was melted over a flame, and a small amount was dripped onto the document to seal it shut. The wax hardened as it cooled. If the seal was broken, it meant that someone had read the private message. Wax seals are still used today for highly confidential documents or on ceremonial certificates such as graduation diplomas.

Unique signet rings were sometimes pressed into the warm wax to complete the seal. The special design of the signet made it very difficult to open the message without being detected.

THE SOONER, THE BETTER

The sooner the nomination is official, the better. Presidents like the Senate to confirm cabinet members as soon as possible. That means they can get to work! Sometimes, cabinet members have been confirmed as soon as Inauguration Day.

PRESIDENT	NUMBER OF CABINET MEMBERS CONFIRMED ON INAUGURATION DAY
Donald Trump	2
Barack Obama	6
George W. Bush	7
Bill Clinton	3
George H.W. Bush	0

The US Constitution (article 2, section 2) gives the US Senate the right to review and approve many presidential appointments. The Senate Judiciary Committee is shown here in September 1991 interviewing Clarence Thomas during President George H.W. Bush's administration.

THE APPOINTMENT PROCESS

CONFIRMATION HEARING

When the Senate receives the nominee's name, it is logged into a book. One of 17 committees is assigned to **vet** the candidate.

Committee members spend a lot of time asking the nominee tough questions. After the committee reviews the nominee's background, a special meeting is held. This meeting is called a **confirmation** hearing.

What does it take for the Senate to confirm a nominee? A simple majority vote. This means that at least 51 of the 100 senators must vote "yea."

Rex Tillerson answered questions from the Senate Foreign Relations Committee during his confirmation hearing in 2017. He was confirmed and sworn in as secretary of state on February 1, 2017.

VOTING ON THE CANDIDATE

During the confirmation hearing, the nominee answers questions from the committee's senators. Some confirmation hearings take more time than others. Cabinet confirmation hearings are usually quick. Hearings for the Supreme Court, however, usually take much longer. At the end of the hearing, the committee votes to decide whether to recommend or reject the nominee.

Samuel Alito (seated, front left) during his Senate confirmation hearing in January 2006, was confirmed later that month as an associate justice of the US Supreme Court.

FAST FACT

A filibuster is a delaying tactic that can include making long speeches. Filibusters are sometimes used to delay a process such as a confirmation hearing or a vote.

If recommended, the candidate's next stop is the full Senate. The Senate debates the nomination. If the nominee is confirmed, the White House is immediately notified.

★ ★ ★ ★ ★ ★ ★ ★ ★ ★ ★ ★ ★ ★ ★ ★ ★ ★ ★ ★

MAKING IT OFFICIAL

At the White House, an official document is prepared to confirm the appointment. This document is a called a commission. The appointment becomes official the moment the president signs the commission.

Inauguration Day Confirmations

Two of President Trump's appointees were confirmed by the Senate on Inauguration Day. James Mattis was confirmed as secretary of defense and John F. Kelly was confirmed as secretary of homeland security.

General John F. Kelly, shown here in May 2015, was nominated by President Donald Trump as secretary of homeland security. Kelly was later confirmed on January 20, 2017. Kelly was reassigned to White House Chief of Staff in July 2017.

OATH OF OFFICE

The president or a designee has the job of swearing in the individuals whom the president appoints to office. These individuals take an **oath** that is written in the Constitution. When the oath is finished, the presidential appointee can begin to work.

> I, _____ _____, do solemnly swear (or affirm) that I will support and defend the Constitution of the United States against all enemies, foreign and domestic; that I will bear true faith and allegiance to the same; that I take this obligation freely, without any mental reservation or purpose of evasion; and that I will well and faithfully discharge the duties of the office on which I am about to enter. So help me God.
>
> Supreme Court Justices and federal judges also state the following:
>
> I, _____ _____, do solemnly swear (or affirm) that I will administer justice without respect to persons, and do equal right to the poor and to the rich, and that I will faithfully and impartially discharge and perform all the duties incumbent upon me as _____ under the Constitution and laws of the United States. So help me God.

Hillary Rodham Clinton takes her oath of office to become the 67th secretary of state in January 2009.

GLOSSARY

administration — a group of people who manage a government

advisor — someone who provides advice

agenda — a list of tasks that must be completed

appoint — to choose for a job or position

cabinet — a group of people who provide advice to the president

commission — a group of people who are in charge of a program or a study

confirmation — approval

consent — to give permission

federal — a form of governance in which power is shared between a central government and state governments

filibuster — a tactic to stall or delay a legislative process

inaugurate — to admit someone to public office

nominee — a person who is chosen as a candidate for a position or title

oath — a solemn promise to fulfill the duties of a position according to law

officer — a person who has a position of power

vet — to research or check carefully

FURTHER INFORMATION

BOOKS

Krieg, Katherine. *President and Cabinet.* Vero Beach, FL: Rourke Educational Media, 2015.

Manger, Katherine. *The US Constitution.* New York: Britannica Educational Publishing, 2017.

Porterfield, Jason. *What Is the Executive Branch?* New York: Britannica Educational Publishing, 2016.

ONLINE

PowerKids Press has developed an online list of websites related to the subject of this book. This site is updated regularly. Please use this link to access the list:

www.powerkidslinks.com/wuwyg/appointments

INDEX